Up in the Sky

by Patricia Ann Lynch

Harcourt

Orlando   Boston   Dallas   Chicago   San Diego

Visit *The Learning Site!*

www.harcourtschool.com

It is morning. The sun is coming up. The sky in the east turns pink. Golden light touches everything. What kind of day will it be?

Now the sun is up. The sky is bright blue, and not a cloud is in sight. It will be a beautiful day!

Some days you can't see the sun. A gray layer of clouds covers the whole sky. The light is gray, too. Rain falls in a drizzle from the clouds.

True rain clouds are very dark gray. They cover the sky in a thick layer and have a wet look. Heavy rain falls from these clouds.

The sky changes from day to day and season to season. There are many types of clouds. Some are thin, and some are thick. They can be white, gray, or almost black. Each type of cloud is a sign of a different kind of weather.

On some days the clouds are thin
and wispy like feathers. Some people
think these clouds look like a horse's
tail. What do you think? These wispy
clouds are a sign of changing weather.

On some days, puffy white clouds float across the sky. When the wind blows, the clouds change shapes. What shapes do you see in these clouds? Clouds like these are a sign of sunny weather.

Sometimes clouds stick together in rows. They look like puffs of white cotton stuck together. Rain does not usually fall from this type of cloud. Rain may be coming, though!

When clouds pile up and grow tall, watch out! These flat-topped clouds are called thunderheads. They bring thunderstorms, with heavy rain and flashes of lightning. You hear the thunder after you see the lightning, because sound travels slower than light.

Sunsets are more beautiful when there are clouds in the sky. Each cloud layer may be a different color. How many colors can you name in this sunset?

The night sky is very clear when there are no clouds. Then you have a full view of the stars in the night.

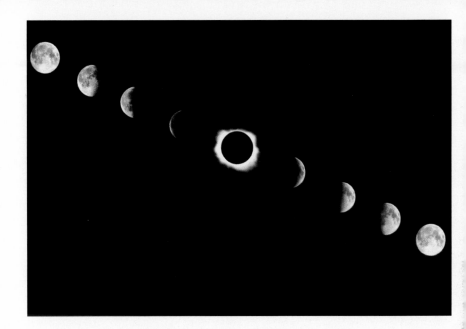

The moon is the biggest and
brightest thing in the night sky. You can
watch the moon change from night to
night. It starts out very thin. Then each
night the bright part of the moon grows
bigger. When the moon is full, the
whole round moon shines brightly.
Then the moon starts to grow smaller
again.

The brightest star in the sky is not a star at all. It is the planet Venus. Sometimes Venus is the first star to appear at night. Then it is called the Evening Star. Sometimes it is the last star to disappear in the morning. Then it is called the Morning Star.

Some stars seem to form pictures in the night sky. These are called constellations. A constellation is like a follow-the-dots puzzle. We call one constellation the Big Dipper. Ancient people called it the Great Bear. What do you see—a cup with a long handle, a bear, or something else?

It's fun to watch the sky. You can see shapes in the clouds and in the stars. The sky changes every day and every night. You will never get tired of watching the changing sky.